INSPIRATIONS & LAMENTATIONS

Inspirations
&
Lamentations

LITERARY DEVOTIONS
OF AN UNUSUAL SORT

ANDREW MCNABB

AROUCA
PRESS

ISBN: 978-1-990685-72-9 (pbk)
ISBN: 978-1-990685-73-6 (hc)

Arouca Press
PO Box 55003
Bridgeport PO
Waterloo, ON N2J 0A5
Canada
www.aroucapress.com
Send inquiries to
info@aroucapress.com

TABLE OF CONTENTS

INTRODUCTORY

BOSTON

You know, when you're born, you're just born into whatever situation you're born into. My situation was good. Not bad. Loving mother, loving father. Siblings. Observant. But there was the wildness of the post-60's 70's. And the excesses of the post-70's 80's. And I was not atypical. And that is greatly my suburban formation. But there was always that longing, which didn't keep me clean, but did make me repentant. Over and over and over again, repentant. And that longing served me well, especially in my young man's ambitions of the post-80's 90's, though there was plenty to be repented of then, as well. But it all seemed to coalesce, a personal emergence from and to, when I walked out of St. Anthony's Shrine on Arch Street in Boston in 1992 and suddenly knew what I wanted to do with my life, write. It would be a few years before that could happen.

NEW YORK

This had to happen first, and I mean, *I happened* into this job. Except I didn't. There are no coincidences, and I had some things to learn. It was early summer and mostly everyone else who'd just graduated from the MBA program was better credentialed and more focused and already had jobs. The company needed someone quickly, and they were Russian just after the dissolution, and so they didn't really know I was not that impressive, even though I was there at that top business school. They hired me.

I wore expensive suits and had a great apartment overlooking the 59th Street Bridge. Yes, there were all of the deals transacted, all the business things learned, the people met, and those experiences unique to that job, like the security in Russia with Uzis, perplexing Slavic thought, needing to navigate the dividing line between two aspiring oligarchs, and the shots of Vodka with an American icon whose company sold chicken. Lots and lots of chicken. A lot of it to us.

But there was that time toward the end, coming to mark the end, the end of the things that at least in that realm, and at that time in my life, that I had needed to learn, when, in St. Petersburg, Russia, I made the mistake of eating a pork chop for lunch in the regular company cafeteria among the proletariat. My boss dressed me down. Someone of my (perceived) standing, he said, should never have done that. Though my eating there was more due to ignorance than humility, it led, not long after, to that last momentous time, over dinner at the Four Seasons in Midtown Manhattan, when I told him I was leaving and moving to Ireland to become a writer. Check, learned, goodbye. And that led, of course, to other times.

IRELAND

Those times were Ireland. Ireland was silent. Silent, silent, silent. Days upon days of silence. And writing. Aspiring word, after purply aspiring word, though written and not spoken, maintaining that silence. Thinking, watching, seeing, reading, reading, reading, writing, writing, writing, drinking, feeling, praying. Walking. So. Much. Walking. And it was green, of course. And gray. And wonderful. And lonely. And seven months later, I returned. And that led, of course, to other times.

NEW YORK, AGAIN

Those times were New York. New York became noisy again. Even if you live there for years, if you spend time away and come back, that noise. I came back to marriage. Marriage to love, sweet love. Incomparable, accepting, endorsing, indulging love, sweet love. A love that makes me feel inadequate given my inadequacy. I am separate, apart, silent. Not unloving, just separate, apart, silent. Though not with her. Though I could be better. In general, like. Because still, I am separate, apart, silent. Though not with her. And while these times are still upon me, certain others have been added to the times, and *these* times will never end.

NEWPORT & PORTLAND

These times are children. I became someone's father on a gray March day in Rhode Island, and then someone's dad (but not right away,) because becoming someone's dad is different than becoming someone's father. It's more work. Seven miscarriages and four live births later, I am blessedly propped up by a love that, as selfless as it is, is not as selfless as it could be, because there is still some part of my *self* in my love for them; which, in a way, I guess makes sense.

And I wrote, and I write, and I published, and I publish, and I sought, and I seek, and there has been a general deepening, which has made this aching longing for Him, always the source of my desire, however imperfectly practiced, bleat stronger, and a metastasizing grace—given, received—that I never knew possible, alongside necessary trials and growth. And here I am.

PORTLAND

And so yes, here I am. And I have lost a dramatic amount of hair, which doesn't seem quite fair given that my fore-bears were not really prone to baldness. But that is my vanity. And after all I have learned and lived through, that I still have an ego means I have a long way to go.

And through it all I have loved You, Lord. Because I love You. I do. But only because You loved me first, and still. And my love is pitiful, of course. But I aspire. And I am not sure what else to do. How to spend my days, except by wandering around, speaking your name, if most often just internally. And trying to love, which I am not yet great at, but I am hoping You can help me with that.

Love.

And it is in this context that I offer these following inspirations, these lamentations.

INSPIRATIONS
&
LAMENTATIONS

LITERARY DEVOTIONS
OF AN UNUSUAL SORT

"*Thy infinite gifts come to me only on these very small hands of mine. Ages pass, and still thou pourest, and still there is room to fill.*"
—Rabindrinath Tagore, *Gitanjali*

TINY HANDS

So, I have these tiny hands. They are expressive. Isn't that what painters say, *The hands are so expressive*, and then they do all sorts of things with hands. How would a painter paint my hands? Tiny, for sure, but that wouldn't tell the whole story. What would? Could anything, really?

As I look at my hands now, my finger bones seem kind of, I don't know, *thin*. The backs of my hands are more Celtic in hue—pink, splotched, blue—than I ever remember, and perhaps older-looking, maybe even lightly shiny from a loss of elasticity, or a thinning skin, or, as I just read can happen, perhaps just *different* because over time the fat in the back of our hands diminishes. Fat in the back of our hands—who knew?

My hands are not like the right hands of my two daughters, afflicted by Cerebral Palsy, and thus baby-soft and limp and under-developed. That hurt I have for them can perhaps be depicted in my hands somehow, but I don't know how you would do it. Some capable painter might. For me, that pain is more of a heart and mind thing, though I know that pain can be good—or at least beneficial—for both their souls and mine. How would my soul be painted? Tiny, too?

My hands aren't rough like a workman's. They aren't smooth like a dandy's. They aren't pronouncedly-veined, as my wife would prefer. They just … *are*. More functional than notable. Come to think of it, if hands are expressive, and if mine are more functional than notable, what does this say about me? I don't know, but I'm not so sure I like this game anymore. They're just my one little set of little, tiny hands, and nevertheless, I will persist, still clapping, shaking, opening, twisting, turning, poking, pushing, pulling, patting. And raising them above my head to the sky. What other choice do I have?

BOXES 1

On the cusp of waking this morning, I said to You, Lord, I offer up my very life to You, and You said to me, *There are many ways to do this*. There are. And only You know which one is best for me. I don't know which way this is. But You do. I do not trust myself to properly interpret things. I am just trying to live; or so I tell myself, because I'm not really trying to just live. I am trying to control.

I love you, Lord, and my goal is to live Your will for me. Here I am. You brought me into this world to love. This is what I want to do. Yet I don't.

I sat down here to figure things out. But figuring out is really not up to me. If I don't see it, it doesn't mean it's not right there, already figured. I know and sense the veil. You are here, and You are there. On this side of the veil, I move about. We all do. I've got this situation. My situation. You know my situation. You've known it all along. And while You know my situation, I'm still trying to figure it out. It's fool's work, but only because I'm a fool. I know You are teaching me something, and I am only beginning to catch on. I am so bound, but only because of myself; but maybe not quite so, there is learning in endurance.

I tell myself to remember: I haven't done anything wrong, I haven't taken any wrong approach (except all of the many, so very, very many obvious and not so obvious ones.) I am exactly where I am supposed to be. If I have separated things into boxes, Lord, it is a human way to help me cope. I simply want to be with You. If there is anything holding me back, it's me, and so I need You, and so what You are saying, if I am hearing correctly, is that I need to just keep moving about, and keep breaking down all these boxes. But I'm the one who just said all this, all you said was, *There are many ways to do this*.

ALL BUSINESS

Going and getting an MBA was no less seeking Him than seeking Him on my knees or in the pew, it was just that I didn't know it was Him whom I was seeking. I mean I did, but I didn't. A true understanding of what it means to be human is understanding why it is we seek. We seek because we are separated from that which we long for. Often, we don't realize that what we long for, ultimately, is Him, and so we insert other (often good) things as replacement, while not recognizing He enables us to strive for those things and is even *present* in those things, but those things can never fully satisfy. So, my striving for that MBA was really my striving for Him, for what only He can provide, but because I only saw pie charts and case studies and group work and networking and not Him in those pie charts and case studies and group work and networking, I was a miserable young lad. Maybe not entirely miserable but, perhaps, *out of place*. I went into that program seeking Him, but not realizing it, so not finding him, but finding pie charts and presentations, case studies and group work, and I wasn't really looking for that, but for Him. Except I didn't know it. The thing is, while the MBA program was not Him, *He was still actually there*, and if I had only realized that, maybe things would have been different.

ON ROLLING UP & DYING

And this is why, in short: my wife told me about a man she saw today at the shoe store at the Mall who could not control one of his eyes. One eye stayed the course, the other rolled straight up, repeatedly. I hadn't witnessed or heard of that particular affliction before. In my years, I have come across the wall eye, the cross eye, the missing eye, even the cat eye. Not to mention all those other lesser ocular afflictions—the pink eye, the red eye, the dry eye—of that "portal to the soul." Portal to the soul, indeed.

But this man, search for me a greater tragic hero in all literature. Their tragedies, at least, had the mark of monumentalism, whereas this is merely a quotidian suffering, an anonymous suffering, a suffering, largely, of unchosen waywardness. Or maybe he is not suffering at all? Maybe the issue is with me. Maybe I am to see it simply as *diversity*. Diversity of eye, to be ignored, or as we are instructed these days, to *not see it* at all.

I am not cynical. And I have no idea how that young man feels about his situation. I do not underestimate the power of character, of resilience, of self-confidence, of perspective. Of wisdom, of counsel, of understanding, of fortitude, of knowledge, of piety, of awe of the Lord. Of grace. It is just that I am weak. And foolish. And self-conscious. And I don't know how I would handle such a thing in my own life. Could I really be on display for fools like me to ogle? And when I'm pricked—for me, for someone else—I just feel like rolling up and...

EVER ANCIENT, EVER NEW

I am not an historian. I am not an intellectual. I am not particularly great at anything as my wife and kids will tell you, but I see that His beauty is ever ancient, ever new.

My hair is going, my teeth aren't great, I don't have a ton of money, but I am comely enough and wealthy enough to see that His beauty is ever ancient, ever new.

I am jaded. I am blinded. I am weak me, both unfortunately, yet fortunately, for He is He, and I am, but not because of me, and so I see, because my given eyes are open enough to *know* that His beauty is ever ancient, ever new.

JUST MAYBE

Maybe I *do* have an obsession with wrongly-rooted excep-
tionalism. Maybe my focus *is* a result of an ego-driven
striving. Maybe my nattering and nagging them *does* have
a root in how I feel *I* will be perceived based on their
accomplishments. Maybe that constant looking about *is*
to gauge how things are measuring, matching up. Maybe
that anxiety *does* have more to do with fear about being
left behind than about being driven. Maybe my comments
do have more to do with envy than sympathy than I
thought. Maybe my saying I don't buy in *is* just a defense
mechanism in case things don't work out. Maybe I like it
when people fail, or things don't work out, or I surpass
someone else in whatever way, in addition to all the good
and devoted and selfless things I do. Just maybe.

PURISH

How does one live pure? We do agree this is the goal, right? Or maybe it isn't. I have been hearing that pure is unattainable; so is pure, then, *not* the goal? Is there a replacement goal? Some measure of gray smoking through the pure? How much? How many wisps at a time? How dark their color? Do they plume forever or do they settle, gray upon gray making black; or, at least, that mottled, dead-looking gray. I am thinking of the gray of that rotten lung I once saw in a textbook, the one there to keep kids from smoking. So then, is a rotten lung of a life really not so bad after all given that it is perhaps more reasonable? Is mottled gray the new black (or, should I say, white?) Is pure in the lung of the beholder? Right, maybe we have it all wrong. Perhaps the question should be, Why pure? Because further, What *is* pure? And because even further than that, Who gets to define it? You? Me? They? Maybe a new word for pure could be constructed. Purish. I vote for purish. Purish is the goal. So I guess the question would be, How does one live purish? We do agree this is the goal, right? Or maybe it isn't. I have been hearing that purish is unattainable...

QUIETUDE

What else is there but quiet? When we just sit and *know*. Or when we just sit and are *given* to know. Properly ordered quiet is at least some sort of acknowledgment, some form of gratitude *lived*. It is essence. In a state of *quietude*, I can come up with things like, The sky is His, a portal to Him, a reminder of His magnificence, His promise, His boundlessness. Or, maybe, The sun is of God, and so when you are lying on the beach you are not basking merely in the sun but also in Him. It gives getting a tan, or even a burn, a whole new meaning.

But does it? Something that has a deeper meaning doesn't *not* have a deeper meaning just because you can't see it. If you don't recognize the sun is *of* Him, the sun is no less *of* Him, it is just that you are missing out on *Real*. And why would you want to do that? Otherwise the sun is just a hot disc in the sky, when that's not really *only* what it is at all.

WHICH IS IT

I don't care about this house. I don't care about this car. I don't care about this vacation that I can't afford to take.

I care about this house. I care about this car. I care about this vacation I can't afford to take.

I don't care about how I look. I don't care about how they see me. I don't care about how I match up.

I care about how I look. I care about how they see me. I care about how I match up.

Depends on the day. Or even the hour. But I know not the day. Nor the hour. So care. About not caring.

MUTENESS TO MEEKNESS

God has not given us a mute life, but one bound for expression—even noisy expression, maybe even cheering. Yes, there can be muteness even if one cheers. Even if one loves some game or other and cheers. Loudly. An entirely noisy life can be (should be) composed in muteness. Peace. That inner cell, mute but so expansive, so expressive, always available, where this or that importantly quiet loudness is recognized. Muteness.

And muteness is that entrée to meekness, which may not be what you think it is; what it is is healing; healing of the idea that we can achieve anything by our own effort or that we know best what should be done, how to cheer, how loudly, how softly, and maybe even what to cheer for. Meekness.

So, muteness to meekness *in* muteness *because of* meekness. And remember what has been written, that the meek shall inherit the earth. And we all know how noisy *that place* is.

SOLITARY

Solitary, not solitaire~y. Solitaire is a game, beautiful in its own way (because it is solitary), but much less con~sequential. Whereas solitary is serious. And much more salutary. Because really, truly, that is what you are, solitary. Are you not? Are you together, or gathered or conjoined at your essence? No, you are solitary. Alone. If not quite *left* alone. And because you are solitary, yet not quite left alone, you are responsible for the state of your solitari~ness. So solitary is not a game but it doesn't mean the stakes aren't high.

THE PLAN

Okay, so, what's the plan? According to Drake, it's God's Plan. According to Jayson Tatum, it's Gods (sic) Plan. According to lots of people — me included — it's God's Plan. Lots of other people say it's not God's plan, that there is some other plan, or no plan at all, or just go ahead and plan it on the fly, or do, indeed, plan, but plan *your* plan. But I think Drake and Jason Tatum have it right. It's God's Plan. So, what *is* that plan? I really want to know. Except I know that I can't know. At least not everything. But I do know some things. Actually, no, I do, in fact, know everything. Or at least every important thing. How? He actually *gave us* the plan, and my Kindle tells me it will only take two-hundred-thirty-four hours to read (NABRE, anyway.) The only thing with that plan is, *am I going to cooperate?*

SO MUCH

I have experienced the sob-inspiring selflessness of human goodness, so plainly straightforward, so beyond within. I have experienced the dysfunctional evil of man's twisting depravity, inflicting, inflicting. I have experienced a mite of Him, Himself, deigning as He did my leveling, my hollowing, sowing a whole new world. I have experienced spiritual evil, pathetically haunting, yet diabolically helping. I have experienced the natural, this immensity of impossibility, so multi-hued, so pointed, so soft, so wet, so *so*. I have experienced the calming satisfaction of the daily, the supposed routine, this undulation of the bigness of the smallness, where everything has import, everything has meaning, where nothing comes or goes without a ripple. And it is all a blasting overload. It is all so much, so very blessedly much, so much to handle, so very, very much to handle. Everything, all of it, so very, very much to handle.

THIS, THEN THAT OR THAT

This lonely, bedraggled, exalted, confused experience.
This pierced, noble, distraught, pleasing minefield.
This disgusting, kind, awkward, angry surprise.
This melancholy, splendid, vexing, deep expedition.

...then...

That wicked, angry, malevolent, burning resentment.
That acrid, sulfurous, tedious, furious position.
That obsessed, looping, frantic, grim abhorrence.
That biting, griping, loathing, dreary provocation.

...or...

That euphoric, perfect, light, easy float.
That ecstatic, buoyant, luminous, reverent harmony.
That thrilled, radiant, knowing, bright reconciliation.
That stunning, startling, prodigious, quenched contentment.

MAN OF SORROWS

He was a Man of Sorrows. Sorrowful, indeed. So sorrowful that it had all come to pass, this. So sorrowful that He was here and she was there, yes. Now, and now forever, so. She was lovely. She had been just so lovely. But what was He to do now? He had done all He could do. It was up to her. It had been up to her. She could have done something. She did do something, really. Many things, in fact. Her life had been full of many, many things. While He waited. So many, many things. Most of them, He would say, were sorrowfully inattentive to the true beauty of true sorrow. And so not only was He a Man of Sorrows. He *is*, because of what she could have been. Many, many sorrows, indeed.

SICK

St. John the Evangelist wrote: *The one whom thou lovest is sick*. And so it is so and such a given that *this one* whom thou lovest is sick. Mm-hmm, *love*sick. I take this walk every day. There is a patch of woods across the street. It's not big, but it doesn't have to be. Just big enough so I can't be seen. If I can't be seen I can do whatever I want. What I want is to walk, of course, but also to just stand. And so I stop and stand. Frequently. When I stop and stand, I pray. Sometimes by speaking, but mostly by simply looking. Bark knots, squirrel nests, lichen. Why are those contours so pleasing? Aren't those sciuridae industrious? And there you are again you impossibly-flat-and-hazed-mellow-blue-green fungus clinging to that doline ledge. I don't care that there is a chain link fence behind me marking trespassing for the quarry. I don't care that there's a highway humming in the distance, and a dog barking somewhere nearby; there's birds, and I can't be seen. I trudge and I stand. I trudge and I stand. I look up. I pray, a lovesick soldier, but so much more fortunate, not having to wait to see his sweetheart.

SICK, TOO

And so it is so and such a given that I am that other
sick, too. The sick the one whom Jesus loved wrote about.
Yes, I am both; the lovesick, the spiritually sick. But the
one sickness can actually make well the other. You see,
the catastrophically downed trunks, the dropping leaves
spinning, the vernal pools that stretch into autumn, even
winter, heal by what they reveal: bigness. That other sick,
the immoral, corrupt, weak, foolishness can inspire thirst
for healing by what it reveals: smallness. The bigness, my
smallness. Divine Physician, heal me.

POKE

I am a big fan of that bumper sticker, "I like poetry, long walks on the beach, and poking dead things with a stick." It's the best. Who are you who wrote it? Call me. Let's laugh. I came up with a few of my own to share: "I like Mary, Immaculate, Joseph her most chaste spouse, and the supermarket donuts served in the narthex after Mass." And, "I like plenary indulgences, going on pilgrimage, and touching the water scum that forms in the holy water font at the entrance to the church." And, "I like the risen Christ, anything pneumatic, and seeing the depleted, ageing population at a once thriving parish." Wait...

DRY BONES

Sometimes when I pull a chicken bone away from my mouth and add it to the pile, I look at what I've done. The carnage. Savage-like, with the teeth and such. And just so you know, I feel no compunction. None. Though I just sucked and chewed meat off a bone, it's like *whatever*. It was basically a product. But that pile of bones. Perhaps a different story. No, no, those chicken bones are done, son. Let'm dry. Aridify. And we're all just a bag of bones, right? Ossified. *Osteoblasted!* And so no, I'm not thinking at all about that condition, *osteogenesis imperfecta*—brittle bones—that I've been seeing all around me, at least under a spiritual skin. Dry, dry. So dry you can taste the dust, feel it blow past those nose hairs and right on up and in as you walk throughout this valley. God, it was Ezekiel you told to speak to the bones, not me. *Speak to the bones, Ezekiel,* You said. *Say to them, Dry bones, hear the word of the Lord!* But those were human bones, not chicken bones, and I just want to eat. Little wings in a pile, be not my memento mori!

DRUNK

"You know what?" I said to my son. "It's tough being your age." He nodded.

"You know what, too? It's tough being my age, having someone your age." He nodded, though he clearly didn't take the time to go too deep with that. Dad talks like this. I try not to overload.

What I didn't say—this time anyway—was it's because I know what sin is now. It's not that I didn't know what sin was then, thanks be to God. It was just that I couldn't control myself, except that I could; I just chose not too because I was, well, his age. And that's not an excuse, just an explanation, because it's kind of like, you know, a thing, being young and dumb and not good at controlling yourself. It's not new. Even the Psalmist pleaded, "Remember not the sins of my youth." But I know the ravishment. Young, old, it matters not. Ravishment. Utter ravishment. I know the utter ravishment of sin. My question: How much of an allowance does God make for age?

When I was that age, I was, among other bad and sinful things, straight drunk. Regular drunk. Drunk on being drunk. Drunk on being dumb. Dumb on being drunk. Drunk. Which doesn't mean I think it's okay for him to be drunk. But I understand why he would want to be drunk, even though he doesn't seem to quite have my inclinations, blessed be God and thanks be to His Holy Name. But he's still young. And it's not really about me at my age, having someone like him at his age. It's purely about him. And about Him. And about sin. And about separation. And I worry about it. And so I don't want him to be drunk.

DECISIONS

No, He wants me to be happy. Yes, He wants me to be happy.
Yes, He wants me to be happy. No, He wants me to be happy.
No, He wants me to be happy. Yes, He wants me to be happy.
Decisions.

LAMENTMENT

What is this? What is this You are allowing to happen? And for how much longer? Why do I see the benefit, yet the futility of it all? Why do I even see it at all, when so many seem to not. But some do, maybe even He/Him, or She/Her, or even They. Maybe they sees it, maybe they doesn't see it, I don't know. Maybe they sees some new better *this*. Maybe I just don't.

MAKE A MESS

Go out and make a mess. Hm. Well maybe I *have* made a mess of it, without hardly trying. And maybe I *do* make a mess of it, it just comes naturally. Why should I *try* to make a mess? I don't even need to do that, to try to make messes; in fact, I'm trying to *clean up* messes, thank you very much.

CAP TOE OXFORDS

I remember so vividly this one time in Washington, D.C. nearly twenty-five years ago when I spent a glorious hour or so just walking in my Cap Toe Oxfords. I was in an interesting area, near The Mall, long and straight, but I couldn't have cared less. What was important was that I was in between meetings and I was alone and I could think about whatever I wanted to. I remember looking at my watch and timing how long I could go before I had to turn back, and being so *preciously relieved* on my way out, and so *wanting time to crawl* on my way back. It wasn't anything in particular. I had a great and interesting job working for Russians who bought tens of millions of dollars of frozen chicken a month for ship-ping to Russia. And I had just come from a meeting with an important and accomplished lobbyist we were paying to look out for our interests. I would be returning to a dinner meeting at a top restaurant where some such important thing or other would be discussed, and after that I would fall asleep in a bed with sheets so highly threaded I might just melt away. But all of it was just an odyssey of wanting to complete my tasks well because I was anxious and conscientious more than because I really cared. What I *really* wanted to do was walk. And there I was in these Cap Toe Oxfords, walking. And I remember the walk, and the momentary relief, and the generalized trepidation relating to nearly everything in my life outside of that walk, but I also remember the shoes themselves, not just because I still have them and they are my one and only real pair of shoes, and not because they are high-end (*Barney's New York*—RIP), but that they were like leaded weights. Not just metaphor-ically, but physically. So heavy, heavy. So clunky with a big heel. And so bad for my surgically reconstructed left knee. I didn't like walking in them, but I remember

34

floating in them that afternoon. I remember floating on that walk, thinking how I didn't mind walking so far in those shoes at all, what did I have against them, after all. I was free, if just for a time, and *walking*, in my Cap. Toe. Oxfords.

WE ARE ANTINOMIANISTS

[I don't even need to do anything with this. Wikipedia already did it for me.]

Wikipedia: *Antinomianism* is any view which rejects laws or legalism and argues against moral, religious or social norms or is at least considered to do so. The term has both religious and secular meanings. In some Christian belief systems, an antinomian is one who takes the principle of salvation by faith and divine grace to the point of asserting that the saved are not bound to follow the moral law contained in the Ten Commandments.

[Yet, because I can't help myself, I will add:]

Ha Ha Ha! Yup! Except so many of us may not even know that, may not even know so many of us are antinomianists or some mutation thereof, may not even know what the word means or even how to pronounce it, or that it even exists. But Ha Ha Ha, it doesn't mean it's not true! And it doesn't mean so many of us aren't! Wikipedia summed it all up, and so many of us are antinomianists whether we think we are or not. It's all right there! Just read it! Yup!

SALON STYLE

You can put all sorts of things on your walls. Or all sorts of nothing. They're *your* walls. I once had a fancy that I would do up a room "salon style." If you don't know already, that means you cover your walls with framed pictures. To make it interesting, you can have pictures and posters and prints and paintings. They can (should) be different sizes. They can (should) have different frames, of different shapes. They can (should) be hung irregularly, not in a straight line. You may even toss in a mirror or two so that you become part of the display when you want to. All of what is hung can be professional, personal, artful, well-done, informative, quirky—a mélange in your ménage. I actually tried it. I failed. It was all so...busy.

But there is this part of me that doesn't want to. This part of me that says it is futile. That says we are headed for collapse. I don't trust myself, Lord. I need Your guidance: What level of convention in this regard do we accept and live? I abhor corporate activism rooted in progressive, relativistic values. I recognize the greed, and the way it can inspires a foolish and wrongheaded approach to profit. And I have read about and even sense, myself, some evil influence over the ups and downs of the market. I don't know. I also recognize, while maybe not fully understanding, the economic benefit a market seems to bring to society. We do not want to move in this regard in a way that is contrary to Your will. We do not want to be part of something that is influenced by evil. We feel like we can at least partly protect ourselves against this by investing rightly; I mean the Church does this, right? But what is rightly? And I don't really know which to approach it. I just know it needs to be approached *somehow*, not not at all. Lord, I can't live my life worrying about this anymore. Help.

DRENCHED

Drenched. Every moment is drenched. I'm just sitting on a big rock on a depleted hotel property in between basket‐ball games, alone, the interstate not a hundred yards away behind some tough, exhausted trees and you know what? It's drenched. This moment is so drenched I can hardly stand it. And maybe it's the gray sky, which I've always loved, or more likely the strong wind, but this moment is so drenched and there's no reason for that, and that's why it's all the more drenched. Because if I'm just sitting here not twenty yards from a crack‐weedy parking lot on a depleted hotel property with the humming drone of the interstate not a hundred yards away but with a fairly nice green grass under my feet and some clover and some dandelion and it's all drenched, so drenched I can hardly stand it, because He is here, so present, then any time, any place can be. And is. How do we stand it, this being *drenched?*

BOXES 2

And so here is one of my boxes, the one in which every-thing in the world is not as it seems. Or maybe it is, because everything seems broken. The signs are every-where, out and about, around me, and even to me. Broken in a way that seems to demand Your intervention. Well, You are always there, I know, but I am thinking more of a *prophetic* intervention. Or maybe this brokenness is just the kind that needs periodic renewal. Ho hum. I could complain about that, because I would rather everything be fully capsized, because that would mean You would be so near, but You are already so near, and so here I am again, not really knowing my own situation.

DELICIOUS,
WHATEVER THE MEANING

Parousia, Kerygma, Diakonia
Metanoia, Acedia
Proleptic

Apophatic, Kataphatic, Hypostatic
Kenosis, Logos
Vulgate

Via Positiva, Via Dolorosa, Via Crucis
Trinitatem, Sacramentum
Quo Vadis

Bezer, Ramoth, Golan
Pneuma, Praxis
Pisgah

Gad, Gezer, Lod
Gog, Magog
Og

DELICIOUS,
WHATEVER THE WORD

Second Coming, Proclamation, Care for the Poor
Conversion, Spiritual Dryness
Anticipatory

Knowledge by negation, Knowledge by positivity,
Relating to the Trinity
Self-emptying, Word of God
Latin Bible

The positive way, the sad way, the way of the cross
Trinity, Sacrament
Where are you going

Levitical city, city of refuge, city then and now
Soul, Gospel lived
Holy Summit

Prophet, Ancient City, Town of Benjamin
Descendant of Joel, Biblical land
Amorite King

THIS PRESENT SUFFERING

This present suffering is nothing as compared to the self-actualization of that dream job finally landed. No, that's not it. This present suffering is nothing as compared to the satisfaction of sitting in that new kitchen, the one with the progressive countertop and the special drawers that don't slam but ease back into place. Um, no. This present suffering is nothing as compared to the inevitable societal tranquility when we finally get over this ingrained hump of bad within and eradicate all our biases? No, doesn't sound quite right. Wait, I just looked it up. Here it is: This present suffering is nothing as compared to the future glory which shall be revealed in us. *Yes, that's it!*

DISTRACTED

You know how during that recent recitation of the first sorrowful mystery of the Rosary, when I was to meditate on the agony of Jesus in the Garden of Gethsemane, a place I have actually been to, a place where I have actually touched the gnarled olive trees that themselves witnessed that most meaningful, dolorous, momentous event, a place where I actually attended Holy Mass in the Basilica of Agony built over a portion of that holy spot, sitting as I did beside, and even reaching down and touching the very bedrock where Jesus prayed and agonized shortly before His death asking His Father to let this cup pass Him by but only if it was His will, a place where the gleeful weight of demons was surely pressing down on Him, delighting in His agony, brutalizing Him while He suffered under the weight of all that sin, no small part of which I am *personally* responsible for, affecting Him so deeply, spirit, soul, and even body, that He experienced that excruciating condition, hematidrosis, where blood exuded from his pores and any touch at all to his skin was almost unthinkably unbearable, that during the recitation of this first decade of the Rosary I was meditating not on all this but on the Boston Celtics who had lost the previous night and how their team chemistry is so sorely lacking? I'm sorry.

PROVENANCE

Now there's a word, *provenance*. Beauty! Sounds like Provence, that place in France, which must be beautiful, because France is beautiful, right? But then on the scale of France's beauty, you hear about the *particular* beauty of Provence. *Provence. Provence.* It's even beautiful to say. *Provence.* But what's the *provenance* of the word provenance and why are you getting sidetracked by bringing up Provence? Sidetracked? Not a bit. Really, from the tongue's perspective, there's not much difference, a lilt, a curl. An *an.* Provenance. Provence. Provenance. Provence. But okay, then, the provenance of the word provenance. I don't know, actually, but I do know the answer is less consequential than the concept. *Provenance.* Origin. Beginning. And the fact that the provenance of the word provenance didn't really originate with its first utterance but with Provenance Himself. With beginning. With origin. With *Provenance.*

PROVIDENCE

Okay, so the word provenance is not to be confused with the place, Provence, which should further not be confused with the word providence, or Providence the place; but all around, there are similarities. Interestingly, just as an aside, there is a place in Providence, Rhode Island called Providence Place. I have been there.

I would argue, though, that there are more similarities between provenance and providence, than there are between two perhaps more natural comparitors (my word), Provence and Providence. Yes, Provence and Providence can both be seen, experienced. In fact, I *have* experienced Providence; my eldest was born there. Providential? Perhaps. Visitors to both would house the view that Provence is *particularly* beautiful, but I would offer there is a boxy, bricky, plucky, small-city-striving to Providence that can't be denied.

But those are just places. Because He is provenant, truly provenant—*Provenance, Himself*—without whom there is not even the option for more instances of specific, smaller *provenances*, or places, there *is* providence, which means His hand is in it, if sometimes just hovering above.

LIFE

I shudder to think
What I would have encouraged
Had her test been positive
Maybe it was the appeal
In the Lord's prayer
Lead us not into temptation
That saved me
That they now want to change

PARTIALITY

Lord, You are All. I am only partial. Partial, indeed. Partial and thus partisan. Partisan and thus exceedingly partial compared to a wholeness that could be, should be. That partisan is mostly enlightened, mostly well-rooted, but I am human, though I am trying not to be, fully. But that's not exactly true, because what else could I be? No, I am fully human, just partial on my own. But I don't want to be on my own. I want to be part of All. But I am only partial. Partial, indeed.

TO ERR

Not-fearer, Not-seeker, Foresakerer
Not-trusterer, Not-purerer, Overindulgerer
Not-honorer, Not-worshipper, Immodester

Rebellor, Refusor, Rejector
Temptor, Grudger, Lecher
Denier, Despiser, Debtor

Briber, Deceiver, Enticer
Accuser, Flatterer, Backbiter
Mocker, Murmurer, Spiter

Not-proclaimerer, Not-forgiverer, Harsh-worderer
Not-zealouser, Not-hearkener, Hardened-hearterer
Not-testifierer, Not-humbler, False-witnesser

Hater, Babbler, Boaster
Arguer, Judger, Joker
Complainer, Conceitor, Coaster

Drinker, Drugger, Extorter
Fighter, Flighter, Oppressor
Gambler, Gluttoner, Traitor

Not-confessorer, Not-lovinger, False-doctriner
Not-trusterer, Not-submitterer, Fornicatorer
Not-abstainerer, Faultfinderer, Contemptorer

Lukewarmerer.

DYING BY NOT DYING

St. John of the Cross wrote: *I die because I do not die.*

And, *For the longer I live, the more drawn out is my dying.*

And, *the dying it endures ends at last in death.*

And, *Lift me from this death.*

And, *O my God, when will it be that I can truly say: now I live because I do not die?*

Aye. Check. Indeed. Verily. Uh-huh. Yes, sir! Right on. Preach. [Head nod.] [Fist bump.]

Has there ever been a more forthright, down-to-earth, uplifting, rightly-rooted, insightful, emotional, plaintive, desirous, beautiful acknowledgement of the way it is, the way it should be?

No. Never. Nope. No way. Nuh-uh. Sorry. Stop it. Please. [Head shake.] [Sarcastic exhalation.]

LURCH

Most obvious would be the dysfuncted homeless lurch. Like the varietal that just crossed in front of my car at a red light at the corner of Congress and High. Not one lurch, but three. Similar, but different, marked by individ-ual troubles. Stopping traffic, unafraid to be hit. Maybe even unaware. Maybe even wanting to be. Lurchment across the pavement, to get to the other side.

In that lurch—those lurches—is evidence. It is almost too easy to see. That one lurch popped up and down from life's weight. A shoulder bent, a knee taken out. Or life's dysfunction, natural or unnatural, a balance distorted. Or life's bad choices, blurring reason, or rendering a foot gangrene. Whatever it is, it is all on display in that lurch, those lurches, the cockeyed, uncouth, bloated, swollen, aggressive lurches. The lurches of the shouting, addicted, perhaps even embraced victimization. Victims of The Fall. Victims of free-will. Victims of human selfishness. Victims of pandering. Victims of ignorance, and a lack of love. Victims of abuse and mental illness and indifference. And almost certainly, perpetrators of at least some of the above. Victim. Perp. Perp. Victim. Is no one beyond reproach? No. Because I've got news for you. When I got out of my car when I got home I lurched right on into my house. I couldn't help it. I felt it. I had to get in, right? Even if I had chosen to sit, to spend the rest of my life in that front seat, I would sit lurched down, bowed down, weighted, heavy. Victim, perp. Hopeful, perhaps, but lurched. But lifted up, too, not absolutely slumped, still able to see over the wheel.

All these bodies, all our lurches, pressed down, but lifted up, kept afloat, lurching forward, but forward nonetheless. Similar, but different, marked by individual troubles. Stopping traffic, unafraid to be hit. Maybe even unaware. Maybe even wanting to be. Our lurchment, across some pavement, to get to some other side.

WHETHER ON THE THREES

Our Lady of La Salette recommended prayer, conversion, and commitment. Our Lady of Good Success lamented heresy, blasphemy, and impurity. Our Lady of Akita's messages to Sister Sasagawa were pray, suffer, and watch out. Our Lady of Fatima gave three messages to Jacinta, Francisco, and Lucia. Our Lady of Kibeho appeared to Alphonsine, Nathalie, and Marie Claire. Mary Byrne saw three figures at Knock, Mother Mary, St. Joseph, and St. John. Our Lady of Lourdes didn't speak to Bernadette until the third apparition. Our Lady of Guadalupe gave Juan Diego that blessed tilma three days after her first appearance. Our Lady of Beauraing appeared to the children in Belgium thirty-three times, ending in nineteen thirty-three. The apparition of Our Lady of Pontmain lasted three hours, and the apparitions of Our Lady of Gietrzwałd lasted three months. Three days after that first event, the young girls asked Mother Mary: "What do you want, Holy Mary?" Mary answered, "Pray the Rosary daily." *And there's the Holy Trinity, of course and preeminently, Who've existed from the beginning of time.* Israel's three patriarchs are Abraham, Isaac, and Jacob, who were preceded before the flood by Abel, Enoch and Noah. Jonah was three days and three nights in the belly of the whale. Nebuchadnezzar sent Meshach, Shadrach, and Abednego into the furnace. There was a fourth who appeared. Jesus? Some say, Yes. The three Magi presented Jesus—the Way, the Truth, and the Life—gold, frankincense, and myrrh. At the transfiguration Jesus, Moses and Elijah elevated above Peter, James, and John. Jesus's three close friends were Mary, Martha, and Lazarus, and Jesus waited three days before raising Lazarus from the dead. Jesus—Priest, Prophet, King—began his ministry at the age of thirty, and preached, taught and worked miracles for three years. He was mocked for saying He would rebuild the Temple in three days. He was crucified at the age of thirty-three, but not before he prayed in the Garden of Gethsemane three times, and not before the cock crowed three times and after Peter denied Him three times. And this was only shortly after Jesus had asked Peter three times if he loved Him. Peter had said, of course, Yes. There were the three hours of darkness while Jesus hung on the cross, which ended in His death, at three o'clock. He rose three days later. Holy, holy, holy. St. Paul was without sight for three days after he was knocked from his horse. Three times he was beaten with rods, and three times ship-wrecked, one time for three months at Malta. Paul talked about knowing a man caught up in an ecstatic place he referred to as a third heaven, and Peter, caught up in ecstatic place, himself, heard a voice three times affirm salvation for the Gentiles, before being greeted by three men, strangers, from Caesarea to escort him to his next destination. There is the Church Militant, the Church Suffering and the Church Triumphant, and Faith, Hope and Love. God's will is Good, Pleasing and Perfect. And the doxology the Kingdom, the Power and the Glory. And there were the thirty-three martyrs of Palestine, and how St. Peter Claver served the slaves for thirty-three years, and St. Catherine of Siena who died at thirty-three, as did Maragret of Castello, and so many more. And there are other numbers, too, of course. The twelve, the forty, the ten, the seven, the eight, the one, the fourteen. And it's all so beautiful and meaningful. And it's all to be contemplated. And all of it under one big sky where the sun and the moon predominate and where Abraham's descendants are as numerous as the stars. And ... And ... And ...

RIGHT

You can't necessarily make everything all right all the time, no matter how hard you try. I am doing this all day, it seems, trying to make everything right. I have lists of tasks, both electronic and mental, both important and menial. I survey the lists throughout the day, all while making an appeal. But what is right? Really, what *is* right? There is really only one, full right; everything else is lacking in some way, even though there may be a great degree of rightness present. That one great right, the unadulterated right, the only important right relates to Rightness, Himself. You are so laid bare before Rightness, you probably don't even see it, see what Rightness sees. He sees how right you are, how not-right, and if you obsess about rightness, about making everything right, make sure it's about the right thing. And it's really not about having your rightness fully right, it's about how hard you try.

INVISIBLE HANDS

Did you know there is an invisible hand? The economist Adam Smith did. He would tell you that he nailed it, that we are economic creatures and that as long as you understand that and don't inhibit it, humanity will flourish, and not just as economic creatures, but as creatures in sum. I *am* an economic creature. Just look at me each morning updating my account balances in Quicken. My wife is definitely an economic creature. I watch her go off to work each day to support her own creatureness, mine, and the four creatures we are responsible for. But Smith is forgetting something. Two things, actually. Two other, much bigger invisible hands. One that seeks to lift, pat, bounce and elevate. Another that seeks to pluck, flick, slap and dismiss.

Smith would tell you that that invisible hand is actually our base inclinations, or *us*, and in his view we are all these individual, self-interested economies, and there are social benefits and public good brought about by individuals acting in our own self-interests. Not disagreeing, but again, those other hands. They direct, too. And furthermore, in thinking more closely, if Smith's invisible hand is us, wouldn't that mean there are *billions* of invisible hands? Billions of tiny, reaching, self-interested invisible hands? Yes, I think so, and most looking for those bigger hands, invisible, or otherwise, to help get them where they want to go. But not all. Choose right.

MISTOPE

I just mistoped. I wanted to type isn't, and what came out was sin't. There was no auto-correct, and I will take that as a sign. I can hear someone saying that, *I sin't, Father, and I need forgiveness.* Or, *I sin't, Father, and I need mercy.* Okay, that someone is me. I sin't because I do, though I am trying not to, but I somehow still manage. I sin't and I sin and I'm sorry, and I am truly not making light of this. Truly. I know how much even one sin burdens not even just one soul.

Now, further, when I typed mistope, my eyes in my mind went to *misanthrope.* That we even have to have such a word. Oy. And maybe I can take that as a further sign. *I sin't, Father, and my sin is misanthropy.*

God works in mysterious ways. Forgive me.

IRREGULAR

Look, I could have kept going, with having regular jobs and such, and I may be at a different place right now, but I just couldn't. It's not that my place right now is not good, even enviable. And it's not like I do not abide St. Teresa of Avila's words, *May you trust God that you are exactly where you are meant to be.* It's just that I could have kept going, with having regular jobs and such, and I may be in a different place right now. I still think about that different place. But I just couldn't go there. And it's not like I don't also abide St. Teresa's words, *May you not forget the infinite possibilities that are born of faith.* No, I do. I do abide them. And I have seen and sensed and witnessed and felt. But I still think about that different place. Even with all I have seen, sensed, witnessed and felt. Still. But I just couldn't go there.

BOXES 3

And so about that moving back and forth through the veil, or at least seeing through it, or peeking around it. There is a box on this side, a box I stand in. Think of a nice wooden box, like an old-time milk crate. This box is, what you call, *the realities of life*. And everything here, on this side of the veil, at least most of the time, seems very real. I don't actually like this side of the veil, except that I love it, because I am supposed to love it, and there is good reason to love it, but I also hate it, because I am supposed to hate it. He said so. But this hate is not *that* kind of hate, it is more of a *recognition* that that other side of the veil is so much better, and that this side of the veil is so corrupted, and so we are to hate the corruption, and not *be* the corruption, and there I am standing in this milk crate of at least *potential* corruption—the box itself, the guy inside it—that sits boldly at the cusp of that veil. But sometimes, when I'm lucky, a strong wind blows, and that veil blows right into and around my box, and though the veil is still in front of me I get a peek of what's on that other side. I want to jump, but I can't. It's so lovely. I want to jump. But it's like in a dream, when you can't get away, when your legs won't move. But I still have my eyes. And my eyes can see, dimly. *Jump!* Thump.

MORE OR LESS

I need to remember when I'm guiding, leading, instructing my sons and daughters that God, Himself knows what's best, but doesn't force it. I am always, it seems, guiding, leading, instructing, but also, often, forcing. But I don't want to lose them. Now, later. When I am saying to my son, *You should do this*, I *know* he should do it. When I say to my daughter, *You will benefit from this*, I *know* she will benefit from it. When I say to my son, *Do this, you will be more*, I *know* he will be more. When I say to my daughter, *Don't do this, you will be less*, I *know* she will be less, and in being guided, led, directed in all these things and acting on them they all will be...who they should be?

And who am I to talk? Oh, the things I have done that have made me less. Oh, the things I have *not* done that would have made me more. God knew, knows. He didn't, doesn't. He reminds. He has His ways. But He can seem so blasé. Of course, He's not. He just doesn't force. Even if that leaves us *less*. Even if that puts us in jeopardy. Even if we can be lost. *Is this why statues weep?*

I am trying to make everything perfect. I am trying to make everything right. But not everything is perfect. Not everything is right. Oftentimes less can be the path to more. But I don't want to lose them. Now, later. Do I honestly think He does? If He is willing to let them—me—go, should I not do the same? How much less can less be but still be...enough?

INDUSTRIOUS

I do not mind at all the industrial walk I sometimes take on Presumpscot Street. In fact, I quite like it. A relief from the heralding beauty of the woods. And it no less *is*. There is productivity amongst the sheet metal sides and rubber membrane roofs, the oil-stained lots and plows left to rot. Amidst the fencing. So. Much. Fencing. There is power in the substation: transform-ers, lightning arresters, and circuit-breaking switchery. The architectural capacitor bank. And the trucks. So. Many. Trucks. There is one angry truck yard in partic-ular, with its rust-spewn white cement bay house and rubber-rimmed bays, the whole lot of it encased by a chain-link warning. That warning is barbed, and the contradictory fatalism comically bleats, because despite a razor-sharp reason for not wanting you in, one sec-tion of fence has lain garbled on the sidewalk, off its tilting posts, for months. And everything here is boxy. Everything. Some of the boxes have names that are boxy themselves — *Apex Industries*, *Mechanical Services* — seem-ingly intentionally to obscure what might be going on inside. The message? Here, we work. Don't ask. And it goes on. And on. And there is so much to see. And it is not depressing at all. There are many tints. One of them is yellow. This forlorn taxi company lot. Uber has done you dirty, Taxi, yet here you still are, and this lot is perhaps a good and fitting spot to sulk; yet your yellow is hopeful. Hopeful. And all this is set to the tone of the constant accelerated whiz to just get through it. An apocalyptic autobahn. No one really cares. There are no *Drive As If Your Children Lived Here* signs, because no children live here. This is a place for adults, and I am an adult, enjoying all of it and how it is garnished. The bottle caps. The rum bottles. The gritted, pounded clothing. The metal bits. The plastic. The toughened carcasses of urban creatures hit and limped to the side. And sand underfoot. So. Much. Sand. But it is all, still, bright in its own way, just differently abled, and He is no less here than anywhere else, which means this walk is just as beautiful as beautiful can be.

THE CLOUD OF IGNORING

I think so many of us are pretty much all caught up in a cloud of unknowing. This is not to be confused, of course, with *the* Cloud of Unknowing, that anonymous work of Christian mysticism written in Middle English which draws on Pseudo-Dionysius the Areopagite and Christian Neo-platonism and focuses on the *via negativa* road to discovering God as a pure entity beyond any capacity of mental conception and so without any definitive image or form (thanks, Wikipedia.) No, I think so many of us are pretty much caught up in, like, a regular cloud of unknowing.

You know how some people say, *You don't know what you don't know.* Well, that's one form of unknowing. They were never taught and so they don't know. Not everything that you should know, though, has to be taught. I would say the most important things to know are actually *already known*, are ingrained, but need to be developed and explored but are ignored because we are too busy, or too distracted, or it seems too hard, or not that fun, or someone said, *Don't go there.*

But there's another type of unknowing, and it's even more unfortunate. You know how some people say, *I wish I could unsee that?* They've seen something, but they wish they hadn't? Well, many of us have been taught things—important things, the most important things, *Truth,* even—and are saying, *I wish I could unknow that.* And you know what? They're doing a good job of it. We have unknowed quite a bit. Or maybe, if not quite unknowed, ignored. Yes, ignored, because we are too busy, or too distracted, or it seems too hard, or we have our own opinions on it, or we only like part of it not all of it, or it's not that fun, or someone said, *Don't go there.* Maybe it should be the cloud of ignoring. Yes. So many of us are pretty much all caught up in a cloud of ignoring; maybe even *the* Cloud of Ignoring. And it's dark.

DOG DAYS

You are dogmatic
    Well you are dissolute
You are dogged
    Well you are dithering
You write doggerel
    Perhaps
God damn it!
    Doggone it!

BETTER

Is today really that much better? Back then they hung Him on a tree, true, but today they do pretty much the same, just with different types of nails and wood. And they is we, really. And it's not just Him, it's us. And it's not just back then, it's sooner than back then. Are we, today, really that much better? Are things, today, really that much better? Is life, today, really that much better? Is there more dignity, less suffering? Is there more opportunity, less anguish? Is there more devotion, less ignorance? Is there more happiness, less sadness? Is there more peace, less anger? Is *Ireland* better? Tell me, is *Ireland* better?

DROOP

St. Paul said, "Strengthen your drooping hands" (Heb 12:12).
Imagining it. Drooping hands. Hm. Paul didn't done got
it there himself, though. Isaiah, Sirach and Job beat him
to it (35:3, 25:33, 4:3). So, if Paul was still talking about
drooping hands all those centuries later, might drooping hands be a human condition? Humans are humans.
Might the same dumb, bad, drooping inconstancy from
way back be pretty much the same dumb, bad, drooping
inconstancy today? You've heard it, history repeats itself.
Not that I need much convincing. I see lots of drooped
hands around me (oftentimes at the end of my own wrists),
looking a lot like those Salvadore Dali watches. How do
we pick up anything? But maybe it doesn't end just there.
Strengthen your drooping feet, today's Paul could say. *And*
your elbows. *And* maybe even your shins and your collar
bones. Your hips. Ankles. Just stiffen it, stiffen it all up!
You're drooping!

PROSPERITY GOSPEL

Who, exactly, is prosperous? What, exactly, is prosperity? What would you do to be prosperous? What would you not do to not be? What would it prosper you if you were to gain the whole world but...? What does it *really* mean to expand, boom or burgeon? What is lucre? Flourishment? The good life? How about to do all right for yourself? To be in clover? To get ahead? To blossom? What does it mean to blossom? No, seriously, what does it mean to blossom, to do you, to live your best life, to follow your passion, to follow your dreams, to let no one and nothing stand in your way? Or to excel, to exceed, to get ahead? What does it mean? *What does it all mean?*

HIGHER ED

Here. You. Go.
Here. Is. Your. Higher. Ed.
Here. Your. Mind. Will. Get. High.
What. Happened. To. The. Old. College. Try.

THE FLOW

The mail room worker in *Elf*, in a moment of drunken self-reflection, says to Buddy, "I need to get into the flow." Buddy, dutiful friend and, above all, *modern man*, considers his friend's emotional desire and without hesitation, without further thought, agrees, repeating, "You need to get into the flow."

But then it happens. Almost instantaneously. As if angels descended. Awakened. The scales still falling from his eyes, the mail room worker rebukes *modern man* for his simple going-along, "*No!* I need to get *out* of the flow! The flow is what got me in here!"

The flow. That presumed positive. That unquestioned current, which has led this young man *here*, and *here* is a place even Buddy acknowledged the deficiencies and dangers of, saying that it's not in fact *shiny* as promised, that it smells like mushrooms, but even more devastatingly, *here* is where "Everyone looks like they want to harm me." So then I ask the man in his jester's tights, *buddy?*

SKYWATCHER

It's okay to stand and stare straight up into the sky. No, really. I do it all the time. Who's going to say something? It's not as if it's against the law. Maybe against convention. I don't care what they think. But what do they think? Well, most probably they don't think much of it at all. Not many see me. I usually do it at night when I'm out for a walk. I look up. I just stop and look up, straight up, and I am not really looking at the stars. I see them, but I hardly see them. I am looking, but not with my eyes. I'm talking, really, with my head crammed way back, like. It's so beautiful up there, so beautiful. And not the stars or the planets or space or whatever. Whatever it really is behind all that.

DOMICILED

My residence is here in this pretty good city in this pretty good state. Actually, it's just an okay city in an okay state. Depends on how you look at it. I didn't grow up here. Had no real connections here. But we decided to move here, because why not? We're not opposed to moving around. So we're here and so yes, this is where I reside. But where am I, like, domiciled? Oh, the legal question? How I need to have one official residence indicating where I am domiciled? *Domicile*, which traces to the Latin *domus*, meaning *home*? It's a great question, or a question at least, and not as straightforward as you might think. So where am I, like, domiciled? Yes, here. I suppose. According to the law. But not really, because *Here you have not a lasting home*. Well, that's very theological, and not very legal, and very true, and I think many of us pretty much get that, and why are you always thinking of that other home when you are here and you need to be present, and this is your domicile, *this* is your domicile, for now, dude, legally, or whatever. Just be happy with it. But I'm not unhappy. I'm actually happy. Happy. Right here in this pretty good, just okay little city. In this pretty good, just okay state. But this is *not* really where I am, like, domiciled. It's just not. At least I just hope not. Just maybe legally. Because I'm a stranger. And an alien. And it's just...not.

YET

I do not hate, yet. I do not love, yet. Just give me a while.

AND, YET AGAIN

Eternal salvation
But universal salvation
    Hell
But no
    Soul
But maybe
    Social justice
But social justice
    Your secularism is religion
But your religion is religion
    God's True Church
We Are Church
    Your flags
Your flags
    Your stickers
Your stickers
    Your signs
Your signs
    Your Gods
God?

REDUCED

I just became aware of something called physicalist reductionism. Physicalist reductionism is the view
that physics explains everything. It is not that science
explains everything, but specifically physics. According to physicalist reductionism, material things—space,
time, brute factual laws, and various forces—explain
everything that exists. I am just wondering about that.
Not because I understand that, or have any inclination
toward that, or even capacity to engage it, but because
it's so perplexing: this narrowing reduction of bigness
to smallness, somethingness to nothingness, when it's
so very clear there's *that something* amidst us—within,
without, about—so very *unexplainable*. Don't you feel it?
I mean really—*really*—feel it? Don't you? If you just sit
for a while in a quiet room with your eyes closed, can't
you not help but *feel* it?

WORSHIP

They say, *It's a foodie city!* What? Yes. Smoked trout and radish sprout? Of course, and don't forget the egg yolk spread. Come see the kombuchery, the mead house, and the craft hard seltzer. Come here, one owner said, and explore seasonal flavors, and stories from the coast. *Stories from the coast? Do you eat them?* You can do this. No, really, *you can do this.* You can engage this food, this drink with this level of ... *worship?* ... well, careful fella, it can be said you worship that bouncing orange ball, with all your tournaments and talk, all your hype, and all your travel and dreams, with all of your lock-grip competitive foolishness. *Worship?* Watch it!

CORRECTION

I've come to understand there is a good deal more to holiness than simply being correct. That could be parsed. But it's better if it's not. *I've come to understand there is a good deal more to holiness than simply being correct.*

BUT IT HURTS

See, when you know too much, it's not always a good thing. Except it is. Depending on what it is you know. If it's the right type of, like, knowledge. When I knew too much this one time and made a decision because of what I know, it maybe wasn't a good thing because my son was upset with me because that decision impacted him, but he didn't have the same knowledge. Except it was a good decision. But it hurt. Because he was hurt. And I didn't have to make the decision I made, but I made it anyway. And if I had made a different decision he wouldn't have been hurt. Except he would have. But maybe just not right now. But in the future. But he's a kid. And he doesn't really care about the future but about right now. But I knew too much, and so I had to make the decision. And he's mad at me. And that doesn't feel good. So, like I said, sometimes when you know too much, it's not always a good thing. Except in this is case it was. But it hurts.

I AM A GALATIAN

St. Paul said, "O, stupid Galatians!" (Gal 3:1). O, my. But really, Paul wasn't the only one telling it like it is. There is no shortage of some people calling other people stupid in the Bible. Did you know that this—ἀσύνετος—translated from the Greek means "you're stupid"? Well, Jesus, Himself said that.

But I don't think we should be surprised. The Bible is about Truth, right? And if you think about it, from beginning to ending, the Bible is one long story about people doing stupid things—and God's merciful, chiding, patient, imploring, grace-filled response culminating in the ultimate, and I would say, *inconceivable for a human mind*, act of love and sacrifice rooted in the scourged, bloody, humiliated, crucified reality of our faith. All for our stupidity.

Acknowledgement is the first step on the road to recovery. I have a vision, like in a movie, when someone is being castigated and dismissed and there may even be some good reason for it but in an act of solidarity, an act of community, someone stands up and says, "I am *that person*," and then the next person across the room stands up and says, "I am *that person*," and so on until the whole room is standing up as *that person*. Well, I would just like to stand up and say, "I am a Galatian." And just about every day. I am trying to be less Galatian-like, so I can be on the road to recovery, and less stupid. Who's with me?

TITULIS CRUCIS

Not only was there a St. John of the Cross, there was a St. Paul of the Cross. Not only was there a St. Paul of the Cross, there was a St. Teresa Benedicta of the Cross. Not only was there a St. Theresa Benedicta of the Cross, there was a St. John Joseph of the Cross, a Blessed Mancius of the Cross, a Blessed Teresa Maria of the Cross Manetti and a Blessed Piety of the Cross.

There is a Tau cross, a Forked cross, a Jerusalem cross and a Ring cross, which is also known as a *crucifixus dolorosus*, an ypsilon cross, and even a furca. St. Andrew was crucified on a cross like an X. That cross is called a saltire. St. Eulalia was crucified at age thirteen. St. Peter was crucified upside down. St. Paul Miki and companions were hung on crosses together.

There are Knights of the Southern Cross, and Hot Cross Buns. We wear crosses around our necks. We bless ourselves in the sign of the cross. There are crosses here. There are crosses there. Crosses. Crosses. *Why?* Because. It's not just to remember Him, or to invoke Him, or to seek His protection, or to show reverence. It's also for a reminder for something we always seem to forget. We each bear a cross, whether we recognize it as such or not. And it's *that* cross that makes us, if not of *the* cross, then of *a* cross, and maybe even cross⁄es. So you can say it, go ahead. I am Bob of a cross, or I am Mary Ellen of cross⁄es. That just may be the beginning of some day going from *a* to *the*.

DON'T FORGET

Memorare, Miserere.
    Remember, Have Mercy.
Memorare, Miserere.
    Remember, Have Mercy.
Memorare, Miserere.
    Remember, Have Mercy.
Memorare, Teo Oramus, Miserere.
    Remember, We Beg You, Have Mercy.

THE THICK OF IT

The foundation of the world may very well be crumbling, and we may very well be entering into, or have already entered, the End Times. There is really no risk in saying this. John Henry Newman said as much a hundred-fifty years ago. Was he crazy or an alarmist or unhinged? He was just sainted. And Pope Leo XIII? And Venerable Pope Pius XII? And Venerable Fulton Sheen? And even Pope St. Paul VI and Pope St. John Paul II, himself? What I have learned, though, through prayer, personal failure, and the simple reality of the world just plodding along, though darkly and angrily, is that even if this is the case, we are to simply get on with it. Stay close. Eyes on Christ. He'll let you know what He wants you to do. I've been trying.

BETTER BRUISES

Train sings, "These brui⁄ses make for be⁄tter conversa⁄tion."
Oh, yes they do. And who doesn't like better conversation?
So, let's talk. About our bruises. I mean it's nice to talk
about other things too, of course. There are very many
light and uplifting regular things to talk about. Even
talking about the weather with a neighbor. Because it's
not like you can just walk up to a neighbor on a beau⁄
tiful Spring day and roll up your spiritual sleeve and say,
See this big, fat, purplish⁄blue splotch that at its edges
is only now starting to yellow? Well let me tell you how
that happened. No.

But really, I would like to say that all conversation is
of depth. What you may not realize but are also imply⁄
ing in simply talking about the weather is, My fallen
humanity is so deeply wounded that I strive for a con⁄
nection with you, neighbor, even on this most basic level.
I will not show you my woundedness, per se, but I will
good⁄naturedly remark, and with no small relief, that the
sun is shining and today will be a great day. I recognize
your own humanity, inevitably wounded, and I would like
to simply breathe⁄easy with you for this short period of
time, so that I can assure you, and you can assure me,
that all is not lost, and that despite our woundedness, at
least we have *this*.

ON DISPLAY

So, *ostentatio vulnerum* is a thing. It means *display of the wounds*. I think you know whose. To *display* such things, wounds. One on the left foot. One on the right foot. One on the left palm. One on the right palm. One on the side. He rose. Which means all became well. But these wounds stayed. And *that* is why they're displayed.

THEODICY

Theodicy.
I know that.
It is true that.
I have experienced that.
So have you.
That is difficult.
That is necessary.
That is even useful.
I don't understand that.
But I don't have to.

APHORISMIC I

I am having the ceiling in my son's room repaired due to water damage. The whimsy of the exterior peaks and valleys of this home are nice to look at but create problems. Rivulets into leaching ice dams. I can't fix anything of substance on my own, and so enter my contractor. He is a good guy and a talented carpenter, and he just told me his girlfriend's grandmother passed away and after condolences were expressed and so on he looked at me, and perhaps with no small whimsy of his own, said, *We're not here for a long time, just a good time.*

Um...

APHORISMIC II

And a man who works for that same contractor, is just … *sweet*. He is so very… *nice*. Through the course of the comings and goings over the last few months he has always stopped to briefly chat so … *authentically*. Whereas I usually engage small talk as a matter of … *social obligation*. You can tell the difference.

Anyway, it was ninety-three degrees and humid and the heat index was over one hundred, and the crew of four were replacing a three-hundred pound picture window in my bedroom. Struggling, sweating, contorting on a black-shingled roof for hours. It was toward the end of the day and he came into the house after everyone was gone because he had left his sunglasses and I said, *Wow this heat is awful*, and he shrugged and said to me, as pleasantly as ever, *Such is life*.

And his shrug and tone intimated not that *life* was awful, but that into every life some awfulness must necessarily descend. I learned the next day that it was not three hours later that he threw up, was disoriented and was admitted to the hospital for a bad case of heat stroke.

ANXIETY

When St. Paul said to the Romans about married life, *Brothers and sisters: I should like you to be free of anxieties*, I wonder if he was also maybe prophesying about the inverted relationship of the bow curves in the economic chart that clearly shows the need for two household incomes today. I think so. Though when he said, *an unmarried man is anxious about the things of the Lord*, I don't think he was prophesying about today at all. I don't really see this that much. And I am not sure yet about whom he may have also been thinking when he said, *A married woman is anxious about the things of the world, how she may please her husband.* I do know, though, if he said that today, they'd make him regret it. But whatever the case, I think he was spot-on when he warned, *If you marry, you do not sin; but such people will experience affliction in their earthly life.*

A TALE OF TWO BEAUTIES

There is a church in New Bedford that is the most glorious in all the world. Romanesque, massively spired, and composed of rare red sandstone. The sign in Latin above the front entrance tellingly queues up the dripping French Canadian vision contained therein: *The working people of St. Anthony's have built a temple to the Lord.* Walk past the cornerstone laid and blessed at the end of a three-thousand strong procession at its founding, and enter into the light and dramatic. Yes, the torrent of artful evocation framed by Italian marble columns, some lighted with stained glass studdings to give the appearance of precious stones, all of it overseen by the dozens of massive angels, some more than twenty feet tall, and leading, inevitably, to the stories-high vision of St. Anthony and the Child, Jesus together in their loving simplicity as backdrop to the exalted table of sacrifice. Christ is there.

There is a church in Portland, Maine that is the most glorious in all the world. It is low-slung and widely boxy. Upon entering through the standard stock commercial glass doors, the tang of worn rug greets your nose while your eyes are drawn to cork bulletin boards and shiny composite brick. Pass through a second set of stock commercial glass doors and perhaps notice a miniature ceramic telling of the last supper, placed for protection inside an ostensibly donated terrarium or waterless fish tank. Search for the tabernacle...there it is to the side of the altar, genuflect and find your seat on a bench and attempt to decipher the clash of the altar's backdrop, a ringed art-nouveau cataclysm with an appropriately suffering Christ surrounded by stylized memoria of events surrounding His most glorious, dolorous and redemptive passion. Among other things, one such piece, off to the side, is a lone ear. Christ is there.

LAMENTABLE, EXUBERANT
ROUTINE

It's a lament. A dolorous, regretful lament. What is?

Some of it. It's a lament. A dolorous, regretful lament.
It's an exuberant. A buoyant, vivacious exuberant.

What is? Some of it. A buoyant, vivacious exuberant.
It's a routine. A workaday, satisfactory routine.

What is? Most of it. A workaday, satisfactory routine.

NO, NO, NO

No, no, no. No. Not at the end of my life, now. I want to see You, feel You, know You, now. No. No, no, no. Not then. Now.

THE DAILY SHOW

Hello, God! This is ... sustenance. Get ... ready. Have a great ... day. *Hello, God!* This ... here. Go ... there. *Hello, God!* Do ... stuff. How was your ... day? *Hello, God!* This is ... sustenance. Isn't this ... entertaining. *Hello, God!* Good ... night.

RUMINATIONS

I don't care. I don't know anything about that. There's nothing I can do. I've done everything I can do. Leave me alone. Have mercy on me. I love you. I don't care. I don't know anything about that. There's nothing I can do. I've done everything I can do. Leave me alone. Have mercy on me. I love you. I don't care. I don't know anything about that. There's nothing I can do. I've done everything I can do. Leave me alone. Have mercy on me. I love you.

MESSY

But it *has to be* messy, right? There is that stain of Original Sin that fogs us. Messy.

And while there is the Natural Law that is part of our essence along with an innate goodness because we are from Him, of Him, we also have to be taught the faith. But what if we're not? That makes a difference in our choices, right? Messy.

And there is natural human development, the advancement and maturation of certain areas of the brain, for example, that enable us to say, *Wait a second, maybe I shouldn't do that*, or, *Wait a minute, maybe I should do that*. That's a physical, developmental, emotional thing. We can't have that until a certain number of years pass. Messy.

And there is the reality of spiritual evil and its influence, and most of the time we don't even realize we are being moved by it. Messy.

And there are the ways we influence each other without hardly knowing it, and the *We* can mean entire societies, cultures in periods of time, and these may be polluted and we may not even realize it. Messy.

And we are not born saints. Messy.

And Jesus said, *No servant is greater than his master*, and look where *He* ended up. So it *has* to be messy; if not in the same way, at least in the suffering way, and many people see suffering as perhaps messier than it is. I mean everybody has pain and sorrow, but what is it that we do to *avoid* that pain and sorrow, or blunt it? Messy.

And maybe because it is difficult to navigate all these messes that Jesus said the gate is narrow. But many want to say it's wide. Messy.

And if that is a cultural, societal — even, sadly, sometimes episcopal — teaching then *Wow*, the mess may not be seen as a mess, or the perceived answer to address the mess will not be the right one and thus the mess will get worse. There is His grace, of course. And that's no small thing. And that can keep us out of messes. But we don't fully understand His grace, and the many forms it takes, and that He can even guide us out of the messes of our own making, encourage us to use them for advancement, ascendance, but that doesn't make things less messy, at least while the process is being gone through, and at least individually, because you can emerge from your own personal mess but still be in the midst of a cultural, societal mess and how can that not impact you, even bring you down? I think we're there right now. And while there is an ascendant path through the mess, and while it is glorious it is tough work, so many of us do not even know it is there, this most gracious, gratifying, grace-filled, peace-filled path. We need His mercy. And His grace. And we need to pray. For ourselves. For others. So we can all be clean. And not messy. Amen.

DISINTERESTED

How is it that not a lot of it is interesting to me, yet I am not disinterested. I am immensely interested, despite not a lot being interesting. In a way, I feel bad. Let me give you an example. I know these people, friends, who rented a house in a sunny state for a little vacation with other people, also friends. Just considering doing something like that makes me want to—and you may not believe me when I tell you this, but it's true—*cry*, because I wouldn't want to. Not that I was asked. I've sufficiently cocooned myself. But what of those around me, those whom I live with, who might want to do something like that? Sigh. Though it's not like we never do things I am not interested in. We are always doing things I am not interested in, they're maybe just smaller things, daily things. And, of course, there's all the things with and for the kids that I'm not interested in, except I am because I am interested, *so interested*, in them. It's just that, there's so much that's not interesting to me, and maybe those are bigger things, but not always, but I can't bring myself to do them. If I look like I'm about to cry when I'm supposed to do something I am not interested in, my blessed wife will sometimes say to me, *That's life, you big baby, stop thinking of yourself.* I know she's right, and I will get on with it, it's just that there's these other things. And they're so quiet and they're so big, so incredibly, incredibly big, and so intensely, immensely interesting, and so quiet, and yet so loud, even sweetly deafening, and so I feel like there's hardly time for anything else.

CHILIASM

If you don't know the meaning of the word chiliasm, you might think it is a word coined by a millennial.

"What are you up to?"

"Chiliasm, bruh."

Interestingly enough, chiliasm *is* millennialism. Except neither of those two words mean what you think they might: a belief that a Paradise will occur on Earth prior to the Final Judgment.

Hm. Chiliasm, bruh.

MARVELOUS

When you have a monk's inclinations, that sunrise isn't that marvelous, yet it is.

When you have a monk's inclinations, a Summer of obligations isn't that marvelous, yet it is.

When you are contradictory in your life, a lot of what seems obligatory is actually quite marvelous.

When you are contradictory in your life, a lot of what seems marvelous, in actuality, isn't.

When you are marvelous, yourself, there's a good chance you don't even know it, or even think of yourself that way.

When you are not marvelous, yourself, there's a good chance you don't even know it, or even think of yourself that way.

When things are marvelous, beware.

When things aren't marvelous, beware.

Marvelousness is marvelous, or at least can be, I think, because it's a lot like my adaptation of how Fred Astaire and Audrey Hepburn sang, *S'wonderful, S'marvelous, that* You *should care for me.*

WHAT ELSE IS THERE?

What else is there but death and dying? Well, life and living, I guess. Yes, life and living, of course, without which there could be no death and dying. There is life and living, and there is death and dying. But, I mean, *what else is there but death and dying?*

HABITS

Here is, basically, the uniform (habit?). Black ankle socks. Black underwear. Black shirt (t-shirt in summer, long-sleeve t-shirt in winter.) Khaki pants (when going to Mass), black casual pants (okay, sweatpants) when not going to Mass (or before or after Mass.) Black sweater or sweatshirt. Black coat. Black sneakers. Black. Not mourning, just black. All of it covering a scarred, resolved, slowly deteriorating corpus. Thank you.

DESIROUS

We are all — *all of us* — desirous. Right up to the very end. I was once desirous of mahogany panels, though I never actually obtained them. Mahogany panels are rich. They are dark. They set a mood, a tone. They *provide* something. My idea was: Wouldn't it be nice to sit in a warm, dark, rich mahogany-paneled office in a nice old home with character. Bookcases. Dim lighting. Big desk. Nice leather chairs. Not a bad idea. That desire was just one of many.

But desires are constantly changing. I am thinking how now I don't want mahogany panels at all, and as for those bookcases, I had a bunch, and when we moved a few years ago I sold hundreds upon hundreds of the books that filled them for a measly hundred twenty-five dollars. That hurt but it felt right.

Plain walls is now, really — mostly, not entirely — what I want. Plain walls in a boxy place. I don't really care. I mean I do, but I don't. It's not to say that rich walls, or fancy walls, aren't good and don't provide something. They do. And there's nothing wrong with that. Recently, in between homes, we lived for a time in a house that was a marvel. It wasn't outrageous. It was just done well. You could even see the ingeniousness of the actualization of God-given human potential in it. But it was just so...angular. Just so, in a way, too nice. And right now, that's not what I desire.

IT

Just Do It.

Just do *what?*

It.

It?

You don't know what *It* is?

Um.

It is, like, *It.* How can you not know?

It...

Okay, so we're doing this? ... *It* is maybe less something specific, and more like ... *a way of life.*

A way of life?

Yes, a way of life. A way of life where you *do things.* Where *doing things* is It.

I see. So, doing things is *It?* What if I don't do them?

That's your problem. You don't have to do them, but then what will you have done?

I don't know. I guess I am wondering who defines *It*, what those *things* are?

Ughh! Okay, so it's Nike — Nike came up with that line — and so *It* is something athletic and maybe not exactly a way of life but something tough, something difficult. They're just trying to motivate you to be healthy and to feel good about yourself by *accomplishing* something. And they're just trying to sell their shoes and whatever else and you're so annoying! Stop trying to read something into everything!

Okay, so *that's* It. It's just seemed like there should be more to *It.* I'm glad I asked. Geesh.

JUST WANT TO

Just want to stand. Just want to sit. Just want to lay.
  Just want to rise.
Just want to stand. Just want to sit. Just want to lay.
  Just want to rise.
Just want to stand. Just want to sit. Just want to lay.
  Just want to rise.

SO, WHAT IF GOD CAME TO YOU; OR, SO WHAT, IF GOD CAME TO YOU

So, what if God came to you? Or, absent the comma, <u>*so what*</u> if God came to you. That a mere comma can be so powerful. That a mere comma can impact *so much*. In the former, the implications are acknowledged to be so soul-bendingly important. In the latter, heck, just keep it to yourself, you're you, you're not me, you're different than I am than he is than she is; but, I'd just like to say, and to quote my wife who likes to quote Tweedle Dee and Tweedle Dum, "Me is like he is exactly like we is, we of a feather we weather together, wherever we goeses its noses to noses, we supposes that it would be fun for some to be like Tweedle Dee and Tweedle Dum." We are all, in that most human way, in that way of being human, exactly the same. Are we not? You are Tweedle Dee and I am Tweedle Dum. And so, yes, I am just telling you, a comma can matter.

KERATIN

Fingernails were created to be bitten. Or maybe not. But oftentimes they are bitten anyway. I, myself, am an offender. And what exactly am I biting again? Fingernails (and toenails, too, those stout, southerly cousins) are composed largely of keratin, a hardened protein. Keratin is also in our skin and in our hair. This bit that I read stated that the nails grow from something called the matrix. As humans, we are constantly renewing ourselves, shedding, flaking, regenerating. As new cells grow in the matrix, the older cells are pushed out, compacted and take on the familiar flattened, hardened form of the fingernail. This, along with a lot of other things, is interesting, ingenious even. Though, as with much of our environment, and even with our own physical selves, other than eating and drinking to stay alive, we have had nothing at all to do with it.

Some learned soul on the internet also made the point that human toenails and fingernails are "vestigial claws." Way back when, we were clawed, and used our claws for digging and gouging, when there were no tools to do those jobs for us. Some other, obviously learned soul made the point that "the nail also serves to enhance precise delicate movements of the distal digits through counter-pressure exerted on the pulp of the finger. The nail then acts as a counterforce when the end of the toe (or finger) touches an object, thereby enhancing the sensitivity of the toe (or finger.)" And, perhaps more pro-saically, "The nail also protects toes (and fingers) from injury, fortifying the bone-muscle-flesh system below."

And so there they are, this hardened bodily protein, pushed out and flattened, extending and shooting forth ever so deliberately from us, from our matrices, without our hardly giving it a second thought. And so we bite away, or we clip and cut and maybe even seal and paint our wondrous keratin. And it all just seems so normal.

FOR THE LOVE OF
SCREAMING

There is love in this house. Ultimately, great, great love. There is also screaming. My kids scream at each other. And my wife and I scream at our kids. Occasionally, they even scream at us. But my wife and I have never, in our more than twenty-five years together, screamed at each other. If there is a problem, we do the opposite, we go silent. There is great love in our silence. But this is not to say there isn't great, great love in others' screams. Screaming is a survival instinct. Our ancient forebears did it. We do it. Though oftentimes for different reasons. Our ancient forebears to ward off a woolly mammoth, my children to ward off a sibling. There may be immaturity in their goals, and no small amount of selfishness. And so is this what they are doing when they scream, trying to survive? In a way, yes. The screaming relates to an impingement, of sorts; screaming is a way of affirming their desire for life, and dare I even say, Truth. But what is Truth? I think I know.

Much of the time this understanding, or seeking, of Truth is either corrupted or not yet fully-formed. This seeking, at its best, is love. When we scream, we could almost universally be screaming, *I want to be here! I recognize something special is going on here and I want more of it!* But do we always have to scream? Certainly not. Properly rooted, this desire for life, if understood in that best and most truthful way, will progress and will achieve full silence, even if we still make noise. And so it is. Love, true love. A beautifully silent scream.

I LOVE YOU

Perhaps my favorite line in all devotional literature is St. Augustine's, "Too late have I loved Thee, O Beauty so ancient and so new." Francis Thompson's, *Hound of Heaven*, is the exemplar of acknowledgement, profession and contrition, bursting forth after arriving late to the party. But we are all late to the party, really. Right up to our last breath. Their words, and those of many others, have endured. I cannot do better. But I don't need to. All I need to say is this: My Lord and my God, I love you. I love you. *I love you.*

SHRINKY DINK

Trying to shrink, but what I do makes me have to be big. But what would be my shrinking, anyway? A simple life of uninterrupted contemplation? I can have that anyway. I do have it. It's except that my accompanying labor is not brewing beer or making jams but raising these young souls, and being there for that ravishing one. I am already shrinky. Just maybe not in the exact way I should be. And so I dink.

GLUMP AND DUMP

I can just as easily be mired in the glump of Red Sox and Celtics Box Scores as I can in the dump of all the wayward tawdry right before our eyes. That wayward tawdry is so consuming—and so wayward, and so taw-dry—we need these great pastimes to have a break. But true to myself, these great pastimes I turn into little reverential passions of their own. And I have two future Celtics (I tell myself) and so I glump in their personal Box Scores, enjoying but obsessing, yes forgetting for a time the dump all around me, but creating a glumping dump all its own.

EYES ON THE PRIZE

There is a painting hanging between the white marble altar and the sacristy at St. Peter's Church. Jesus has just been taken down from the cross. Martha, her sister Mary, and presumably John (Lazarus?) lament and study the limp, dead (muscly) Jesus. Mother Mary, in blue, *whose own heart a sword has pierced* is aggrieved, but less so.

She is looking to the sky.

PILGRIM

Walking in the cemetery, looking to see how long this one or that one lived. Always excited to see a short, or not extraordinarily long, life. Sorry, but envy. What's wrong with me? Can I be honest and use the sung words of Edwin Starr? *Absolutely nothin', huh!*

Yes, hope and beauty. Yes, yes, I know it and see it. Forget about the major tragedies, the wars, famines, sickness, cruelty, *man's inhumanity to man*, and such; what of the excruciating, panicking poverty of the everyday, so relentless? What of the depth of love that makes the hurt felt for a child simply left off a team so blinding, so bleeding? Are we not supposed to remember that endless black pool of goodness and vulnerability we saw in those eyes when he was a child and *knew* this day, and so many others like them, was coming? What of the middle finger received on the road to somewhere, the tattling undermining of an everyday rival, of the weary drudgery of our own repeated failings, as we embarrassedly confess that same sin over and over? What of the heat? What of the cold? What of the spot of age that just appeared on my arm seemingly overnight?

Yes, yes, I see the flowers. Yes, yes, I know we have been redeemed. Yes, yes, I know we can be dead to sin, can live for Him, for others, and that our joy and optimism can be relentless and rooted and overflowing should we allow it to be—*Him to be*—in us. Yes, it's hard, but glorious, (and necessary) work. But it's work, and even the weary Psalmist noted, *When will my pilgrimage come to an end?*

IN SUPPORT OF A
MORE LOVING, MORE
ORTHODOXICAL FEELING

Pascal (nearly four hundred years ago) wrote, "Those who are accustomed to judge by *feeling* do not understand the process of *reasoning* for they would understand at first sight and are not used to seek for principles. And others, on the contrary, who are accustomed to *reason* from principles, do not at all understand matters of *feeling*, seeking principles and being unable to seek at a glance."

I think, as it were, that what he was referring to, as it were, is, quite frankly, as it *is*. Isn't it? Yes, it is. We didn't just invent smug Traditionalism or wayward Progressivism in this last generation. They *are*. They *is*. We are. *We* is. But how much of each do they, and we, have to be?

PPP

And further, in Pascal's *Pensees*, Pascal formulated Pascal's Principle of Pressure, which proposed and principally propagated passion for a proper approach to...*experiencing* God through the heart rather than through reason. Perfect. Pray about it.

THE GOOD LIFE?

After all, that's a good life, too, isn't it? Working and golfing? And raising children? And trying to teach them the right way to do things? And instilling in them the motto, *Be Kind?* And attempting to minimize suffering by having central air conditioning and a pool? And prepping those young lives for older, educated, productive lives, so that they can, in turn, pass all of the above along? Life?

So why would anyone want to suffer because it is, as some might hold, a good, or even *better,* life? And might it rightly be said there is a certain amount of suffering in every life already? And doesn't our inclination toward self-preservation trend speedily toward less suffering and isn't *that* what's normal? And, I mean, really now, are we to actually ask for *more* suffering? And, should we ask for it, how much suffering is actually enough? And are you crazy? And are you even good yourself? And what is life, anyway?

NEW BEIGE

New Bedford, you are beautiful. Just. So. Beautiful. Yes, all the skin so many hues of beige. Yes, the whales and fish. Yes, just far enough away from Boston to keep you safe from its gentrifying tentacles. But I turned a corner downtown and *this* was there, attached to Police Headquarters. Literally. *This* was a chapel/church, adorned by Mary, so unexpected. Across from City Hall? Yes. So prominently placed? Yes. Walking in, a small lobby, a Friar robed in blue. *Blue?* I am sorry I am underdressed, I am on vacation. It's okay, come in and pray. But who could pray, really, with all the delights. The monstrance, of course; the shining, golden, blue hued (*!*) Host behind glass, perpetually.

[Sigh.]

But Jude and Juan Diego and Faustina and Maximillian and the dripping Jesus and the overseeing Joseph and the Mary many different ways and the candles and so much more, retrolike, and slightly frayed, and not masterfully artisted, and that made it so much better, like New Beige itself, and it was early in the morning and I was high on caffeine and there were a dozen, mostly beige souls therein, adoring. One next to me, though, sleeping, because she, herself, was clearly frayed and needed it and instead of adoring, she was being adored, there by that Host, in that beautiful, unexpected, pleasedon'teverchange place.

PUT ON THE NEW MAN

St. Paul said, *Put on the new man.* Oh, were it as easy as stepping into a suit of new human skin! Oh, if I could be a shape shifting Skrull! Oh, if it could be done as simply as changing my channel, or acting, or snapping my fingers!

Oh, oh, oh!

ABOUT THE AUTHOR

Andrew McNabb is an acclaimed writer of fiction, poetry, biography and memoir. His short stories have appeared far and wide, from *The Missouri Review* to the anthology *Best Christian Short Stories* (Thomas Nelson.) His most recent book, *Walking with Father Vincent*, (Gracewing), explores the life of his great granduncle, the renowned twentieth century Dominican, Father Vincent McNabb, OP. He lives in Maine.

Printed in the USA
CPSIA information can be obtained
at www.ICGtesting.com
LVHW050712081123
763197LV00016B/49/J